WE DANCE IN DREAMS

MUSINGS FROM A HOPELESS ROMANTIC

UDISA DAS

To my first...

And for every heart that has known love: seen it, met it but failed
to keep it.

May you meet love again.

Contents

Contents

Foreword

What do you do with a love that has captured every bit of your being, rocking your world upside down but still lacking a voice? When love fails to sing, it bleeds - soaking pages wet with words that could have been kisses.

But it still exists.

Love is a paradox. It is not rare but again, it is not common. "We Dance in Dreams" is a series of poetry and prose, that echoes the many voices of love stories that could never be. It follows the journey of a heart in love- blissfully, amazingly, hopelessly. The poems follow its passion, its dreams, eventually its pain but its will to love again.

Because, love is too great to be given up for just one person.

1. WE DANCE IN DREAMS

(the beginning)

In the dark of the nights
When the world falls quiet
Our love walks on the piano,
I let out my hand
And yours falls in
And then, we dance in dreams.

2. THE SKY

The sky looks like all you ever spoke about.
It has taken the color of your words.
There is playful yellow
Some passionate orange
And a hint of your gloomy blues;
All synchronized
Just like the perfect symphony of your voice.
The sky reflects the color of my eyes
And all they could ever hold
Was you.

3. THE LAST TIME IT RAINED

The last time it rained,
Our tears became one
And were soaked into the ground.
The last time it rained,
We felt the heat of our burning souls
Clenching our hands
Wishing to trap time
Within our desperate fingers.
The last time it rained,
Another love story
Died into poetry.

4. STORM

When storm clouds sweep over the city
And the world arches its neck backwards,
To feel every drop of rain
Against its face,
All she does is wonder.
Reality blurs out for a moment.
She searches
Through the smudged outlines of concrete
For a mind that thinks of her,
As clearly as she does.

5..

The soul resides fragmented
In people and in places.

6. .

The heart bleeds
In words and inkblots.

7. DREAMS

In dreams
Some rule the world
While some,
Only hold hands.

8. IN LOVE

In love
You do not change;
You reform.
In love
You never own;
You belong.

9. PARALLELS

There are people with whom
A part of us always lives in a parallel universe.
Our souls thrive in it.
We make dinner
Pour wine
And have the best of the candlelit dates
By the window,
Creating a world of our own
In an universe of our imagination.
And dreams-
They hold the door to the portal.

10..

She looked at him
The way one looks at the stars…
Wanting to glance at the beyond
Wishing for magic to happen.

11. EYES THAT LOCKED

And when our eyes finally locked-
Just for that fleeting moment
Just for that blessed second
That lasted longer
Than the years we had never met-
I fell in love all over again.

12. AS THE NIGHT AGED

And as the night aged
My pillow grew warmer
But yours,
Still a stabbing cold.
As the night aged
The nightingale sang sweeter
Just like it did
When we savored the moon;
Our souls melting to the nightingale's tune.
As the night aged
The fragrance of the jasmine
Lingered deep into our room,
Surrounding me with a thousand memories
A thousand dreams
And the presence of You.
As the night aged
You finally came,
To sleep with me
Within me
Leaving your pillow, a still cold.

13. CHOCOLATE

For some, love is a lot like the piece of chocolate you sneak out of the refrigerator late at night. It is like the puddle on the road you jump into, when no one's looking. For some, love does not live in the hearts of their beloved. It remains just as the tingle in their hearts, fleeting yet enormously present. Love remains in their thoughts and in the stars that adorn moonless nights.
And if you ask me, that is the finest kind of love.

14. LOVE

A few glances
A pinch of smile
A bit of care
And a full cup of trust,
Love is not a complex dish to cook.

15. STRANGER

And I will forever wonder
Why we long
For the love we never had:
Why a certain tune
Makes us cry;
And why
When we read characters unite
A sliver of smile
Pulls our lips wide -
Oh Love!
How do I know you
Without ever meeting,
How do I feel you
Without ever feeling?

16. LUCKY ONES

- A Chaotic Thought

People who had a first love, that remained unrequited, are lucky. I envy them. Whenever reality stabs them, they quickly think of a better possible one in which they had their first love in their arms. For example, if one day you get colossally reprimanded at your job, you would think how nice would it be if I could return home and had him in my arms. If one day, you fight so severely with your lover that you cease believing in love and wish to just disappear, you would immediately think yet again, how nice would it be if I could disappear in his arms. And every time in those 'if' moments, you could almost feel a heartbeat, feel the skin you once loved and be happy. A happiness so palpable, that you could no longer tell if it is untrue.

I envy those, who had a first love. They believe in a happiness that can never be real. They have the respite of a fantasy that was once, very real.

17. STILLNESS

When we finally met
All I did was stare.
How do I choose words
From the thousands of conversations
I have shared with you,
In silence and amidst chaos
Awake and in dreams…
How do you greet someone
When you cannot bear the thought of goodbyes?
I was dumbfounded.
I saw the world in your eyes
And found poetry in my stillness,
Flowing in gushing waves from my heart to yours.
Time?
Did it ever exist
Or had it stopped too?

18. SAFE AND SOUND

After you left,
I picked up the broken pieces of us
That loved each other.
I put them
In one of the many lockers of my heart.
Safe and sound.
On those nights
When the breeze feels like the touch
Of someone important,
The rustle of the leaves
Falls on the ear
As the dialogue of two souls in love,
I open that locker.
I see the pieces of us dancing to our tune.
I see us painting love.
No, I don't waste tears.
After all, you taught my heart
To dance.
You tugged at its sails
And I led it on…
An ill-starred voyage,
But still of such worth.
I had always craved adventures

And this was called *LOVE*.

19. WHERE TRUTH RESIDES

The nights are for poets
And drunkards alike,
They forge new realities
Tailored to soothe their minds.
The days are for realists
Who repeat lies to survive.
But what do I make of dreams?
Is that where the truth resides?

20. STAY

And yet how fiercely you have stayed with me
Grasping at every thread of my mind
Whenever they have wandered off.
How enormously
Have you filled every void in me
So much that I struggle to fit myself.
How have you spread to every inch of me
Gnawing through all the walls
That you had erected
And I, ever so foolishly, had agreed to stay within.
I was too quick to ask for an eternity.
I had never known what it meant

21. BACKGROUND

I was always the background

Letting your life unfold over me.

I made a mistake,

I failed to comprehend.

I was only the page

On which you met your soulmate.

22. REBORN

When I see you writing about the last shreds of winter, not just snippets or notes, but poems so deep that they could hold time hostage for hours - longer than bestselling novels or those moments when my eyes met yours; I wonder when were you reborn? Or is it just a whim?

Since when could you notice the subtle glitter at the corner of dewdrops, since when do you see them as diamonds? I read your words again. They reek of the love I always wanted. For us, for me. In these last dying days of winter, I wish to be reborn like the springs that existed. Perhaps now, you would know the seas my heart has chartered. Perhaps now, you would feel the waves touching your feet. Perhaps now, you would write about me.

23. AWAY AND TOGETHER

A half-done song

Our roads could never be the same.
I know,
I know but it is worth the pain.
Let's make a promise, will you?
When all this is over
Meet me where these roads end.
I will take you somewhere,
I have a place in mind
I will take you there…
Where there are no roads
To walk separate
But only the sky to fly
Away and together.
You will come, right?
Fly with me dear, will you?
I promise we won't fall.
There is a lot left to love-
Let me love you again.
Will you?

24. I LOVE YOU

Poetry is born out of an intense urge to say
'I love you';
In every possible form
Over and over again,
In the loudest of voices
Screaming from mountain tops
Overriding the waves of mighty seas;
But the sheer inability to make the voice heard.
Poetry is but an excuse for holding on-
Against all hope
Across every lifetime.

25. HAPPILY EVER AFTER

An entire life can be confined to just that one moment when the heart first fluttered. An eternity can circle back to that one time, although fleeting, when the hands just touched. How does the mind protect that one memory? Why does the soul choose to fight for it, keeping it alive and blossoming even as it, itself craves for a drop of rain? Perhaps because the mind gets a taste of something too indulgent, too precious to be true in a world that binges on reality. Perhaps it realizes that "happily ever after" resides in that one moment - lived over a thousand times.

26. OCEAN

You strike me like the wind by the sea
You tease me with waves
Drenching me in your passion
Carrying me into your depths.
And when you recede
Even though I feel the ground beneath
Sifting through my toes,
You leave me with a promise:
A promise to always return
A promise to take me in deeper,
Away from the shore.
The sandcastle I had built long before
With turrets, a porch
Adorned with seashells and what not,
It breaks.
But what does it matter?
I had only ever lived by a brook.
How could I afford to deny the ocean?

27. BLADES AND BLOOD

I have burnt several night lamps, shifting through pages old and new, millions of them, to finally know what people call love. I have bargained my sleep for an answer.

Why?

Why do people welcome pain? Why do they let themselves bleed, stabbed by the same rusty blade, over and over again?

And yet when I fail on one such night in my never-ending endeavor, I look at the stars that light your skies and mine. I hear stories and laughter. I smell the warm breeze, that shadow of the trees, a very young you and a very different me. And yet I pray for your presence in my dreams...

28. .

I have spent many lives
Trying to forget you,
Only to be dead
And revived the next second.

29. DOTS

The finest of the poets
The most skilled of the artists
Have spent entire lives
Trying to capture
Failing to describe
But only two floating dots.

30. RED AND BROWN

That last hue of red
That last sliver of light
That deep brown gaze
And that last smile,
My heart has never moved since
And yet it races miles.

31. IF ONLY

If after all these years, all this time
I looked at you, fixing us in time
And said, "I love you"-
Would you still run away?
Would you still think me naive
Would you still think me mad-
Or would you take my hands, trembling
Convulsing with emotions
And hide them in yours?
Would you finally look into my eyes
Brimming with love,
Overflowing with truth
And would you finally cry with me-
For the days that we lost
And mourn the nights
That were cursed
To house only dreams?
Amongst the thousands of hands
That have comforted you,
Thousands of smiles
That have charmed you
And claimed you theirs-
Would you finally know me?

32. BLUR

• 35 •

Feelings
Have a way of staying
At the edge of blurred lines
In the glow of faint lights.

33. RAINDROPS

Raindrops are like wishing wells
Falling randomly on the windshield,
Smudging all the lines
Blurring every familiar image
Masking all the street noise,
Until all you can see
Are just specks of light-
Faded yet bright.
Until all you can hear
Are the stories
That you wish were true.

34. THE PLATFORM

Every time my train crosses your station
In the dying but passionate reds of the afternoon
I see you.
I see your house,
I see you standing on the platform
I see your gaze catching mine
Smiling, waving at me.
On some days when the heart is especially weary
You manage to hop on
Before the train whistles.
You breathe a sigh of relief
Realizing you have not lost me.
I smile too, realizing
I can never lose you.
You sit beside me
I keep my hands in yours,
What does it matter
If I feel just the air between my fingers-
I feel you.

35. THE KNOT

There is this knot in my heart -
This burning desire
To see you
Amidst the erupting red skies,
Even though my eyes
Can barely bear the sight;
Even though my heart
Never learned to rein in the floods.
There is this darkness-
My favorite inkpot
And my malignant love
For its enormity, its richness.
There is this awful pain
And then,
My ability to find beauty in yearning.

36. WORDS

I have run out of words
And yet I cannot seem to run out of you...
There has hardly been a day when you do not cross my mind. You live so immensely in me, around me, I have kept you alive. Words have become incapable of describing your existence. Only dreams can do you justice. How do you breathe in me still? Why do you breathe in me still? You bring me pain and yet I cannot let go. Because without this pain, I know no feeling. Without you, I have never learnt to feel. My heart aches from inaction, more than it does from aching for you.

I am spiraling again. Oh but it feels like I am at the center of a tornado. I can feel sleep sitting heavily on my eyes. I know dreams are waiting. I hope you are waiting. For me.

37. BORROWED FROM THE NIGHT

On nights that grow beautifully darker
But only to soften the glaring citylights
I call out to you.
I ask, "How are you?
How have you been?"
I ask about your day
And sometimes the moon.
"Do you see it?
Mine is overcast."
I hear my voice muffling
And feel the wind hitting my throat.
It swishes my questions away
I wonder if I ever made a sound.
I realize I didn't.
I have been borrowing from the night
For far too long.
The wind is soothing
It helps my heart sleep
I don't want it racing
I am tired of the speed.

38. SILENCE

Words irritate me,
Rubbing harsh against the fragile thread
That still connects us somehow.
I find peace in silence.
I let the moon, the night and the wind
Write for me.
They surprise me
Weaving stories where I cannot tell
The truth from cheap fiction.
When did love change its habit?
When did I learn to breathe novels
Without having to relish the smell of new pages?

39. MEMORIES

If even for once,
Everyone has wished
For life to be a poem.
But no one as vehemently as I.
What would I do for a forever with you
What would I pay
Just for you to stay-
If only there was a way to contain the wind
That flutters our hearts today,
I would die happy
Just being your lover
Killed by our memories every day.

40. SCRAPBOOK

As I grew older, I learned to take in people as pages of a scrapbook and not like novels. For someone who always feels more than she should and finds meaning more than what is necessary, this lesson was never an easy one to master. When I was younger, I would be touched by even so little, like a kind smile, a casual pat, or a few lines of dedicated conversation with a stranger. I would wish to see them again, to know them better and also wish for them to know me. I would wish unfolding myself to them and want them to unfold into me. But now, I realize that it would be almost impossible, too far-fetched.

So now I see people like pages of a scrapbook - profound (or maybe not so profound) experiences that made me happy at some point in time. The truth is: not everyone is blessed with the same kind of forever. However, we can always find it in fragments, much like the little stars that sparkle at the edge of broken glass.

41. YESTERDAY

Yesterday
When the night spread stars over the world
And darkness over my eyes
I called out to you,
Hoping you would bring me light
Like you did.
Yesterday
I could not tell you from the darkness.
Finally yesterday
I moved ON.

42. DEATH OF A LOVE

When love dies and we dispose of the dead, what we miss the most is *the person* we had become when we fell in love. We mourn the loss of someone who could be delighted by the slightest rustle of the leaves and moved ever so deeply by an occasional touch. The wetness that soaks our cheeks is not always the memory of our beloved. Often there is an enormous fear if we will ever meet *that person*. Ever again.

43. ROSE-DUST

All this love
That I have hidden in my pages
Like the dead pressed petals
Of a very precious rose,
I hope they find a way to you.
I hope the petals turn into dust
Becoming one with the air
That you and I breathe;
Unsettling it
Displacing it
Making room for love,
Although in tiny little fragments.
I hope it eventually frees me
And enriches you.

44. THOSE WHO LOVE...

...don't ever stop

When you have loved someone for too long, everything around you reeks of them. All the songs you love are because of some specific moment with them. All of your favorite places house their memories. And here comes the pain: the unbearable pain of finding that one person you are trying to forget in everything. Do you really want to let go, you ask yourself. Because letting go would mean you having no favorite songs anymore, no favorite places. "Where would I go, where would I rest;" you keep searching and hoping. But one day you would grow tired when that fairytale love would have become a chore. And the white empty room with no songs and no roses would seem like a sweet escape. One day you would finally throw away your rose-tinted glasses realizing they were but only your tears.

So you try hard to start fresh, start new; avoiding every possible object that could lure you back. And then one day, you would finally find yourself not trying anymore, but just being. You would find yourself enjoying your morning coffee by the balcony, listening to your favorite song and smiling: smiling for whatever is present and not longing for whatever that was never there. Smiling because you would know what you are capable of-

Loving greatly and not just one person.

45. WE DANCE IN DREAMS

(the end…)

The heart can only love for so long.

It gets tired.

It can love for eons and then stop.

Opening its eyes all of a sudden,

It sees the emptiness

That had been surrounding it all along.

I give up today.

Memories have become brittle,

I fear they might break.

No, do not worry

I will keep you safe

Up in that showcase

And I will dust you every day.

I wish you peace and myself too.

Our love,

Or rather mine

Will always remain true.

May it find peace

When a lover rests

In the lap of their beloved.
May it hold hands,
May it see the world
Through another love's eyes.
May it blossom
May it sing
May it finally
Feel complete with a kiss.
I am letting it fly
And find its home,
If not in this life
In the millionth one from now.
Till then,
We will be dancing in dreams
Forever and how!

From The Author

• 51 •

A warm hug to all my readers. I am Udisa (pen name and Instagram handle: @the.penchant), a junior doctor currently preparing for my postgraduation. From a very young age, I have always found solace in writing regardless of my mood: happy or sad, stressed, angry or just simply excited. This is my first book and I hope you have enjoyed it as much as I have loved writing it. Much like almost everything in this world, love can be very complicated and difficult to navigate. But I hope that my words have brought you some respite. I wish for you to enjoy love just for love's sake.

Till we meet again,

Udisa Das
August, 2024